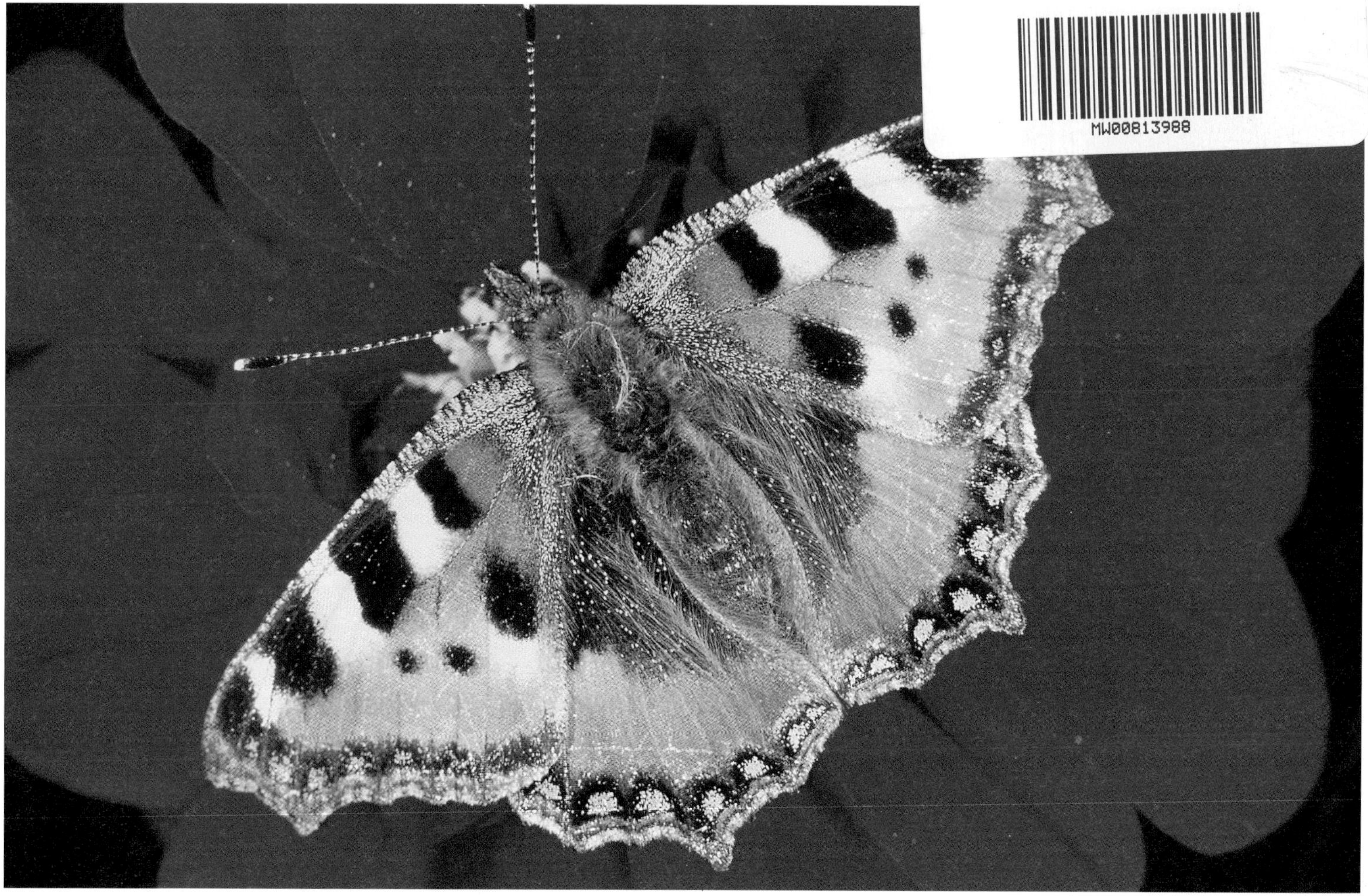

butterfly

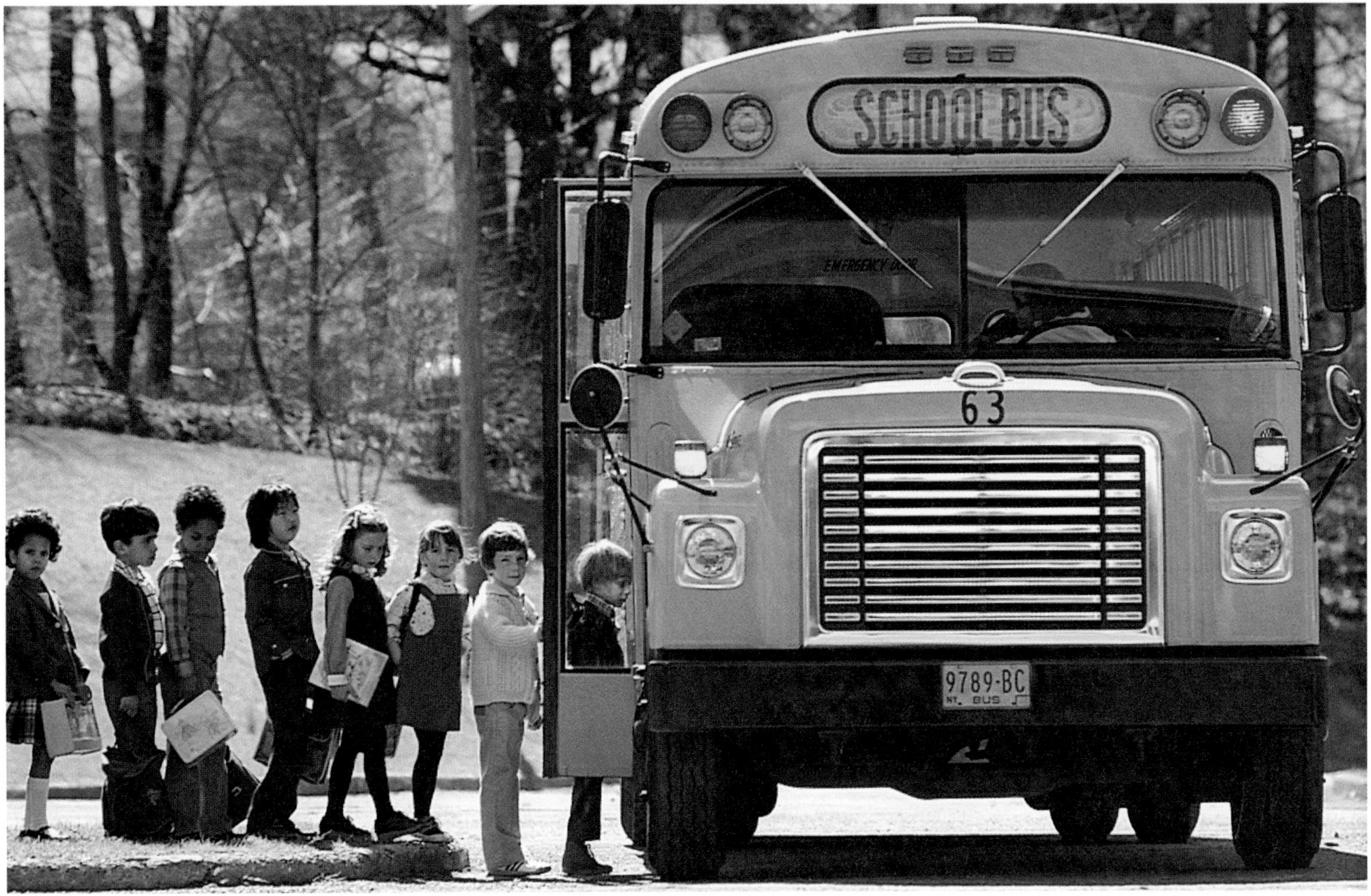

bus

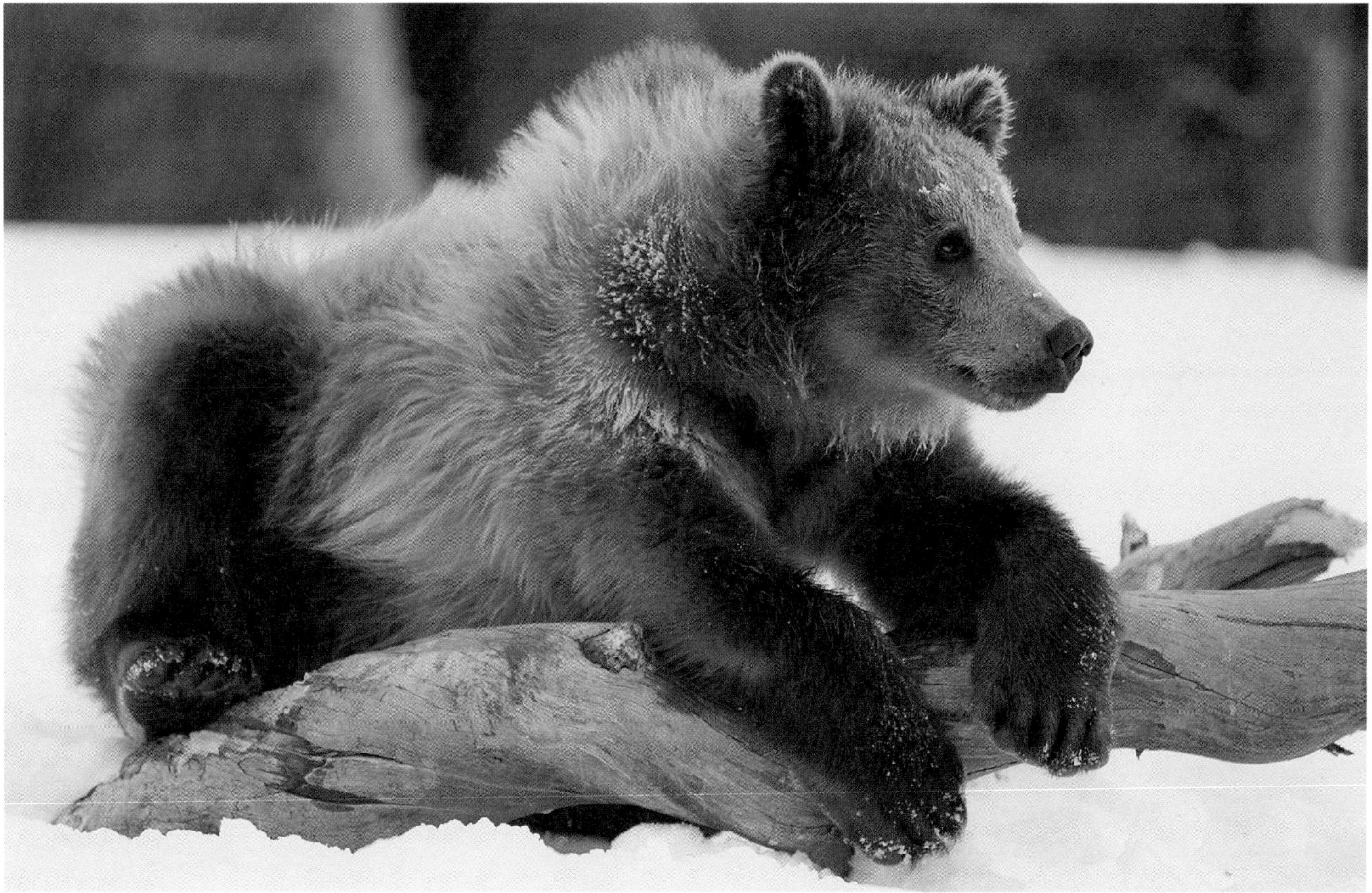

bear

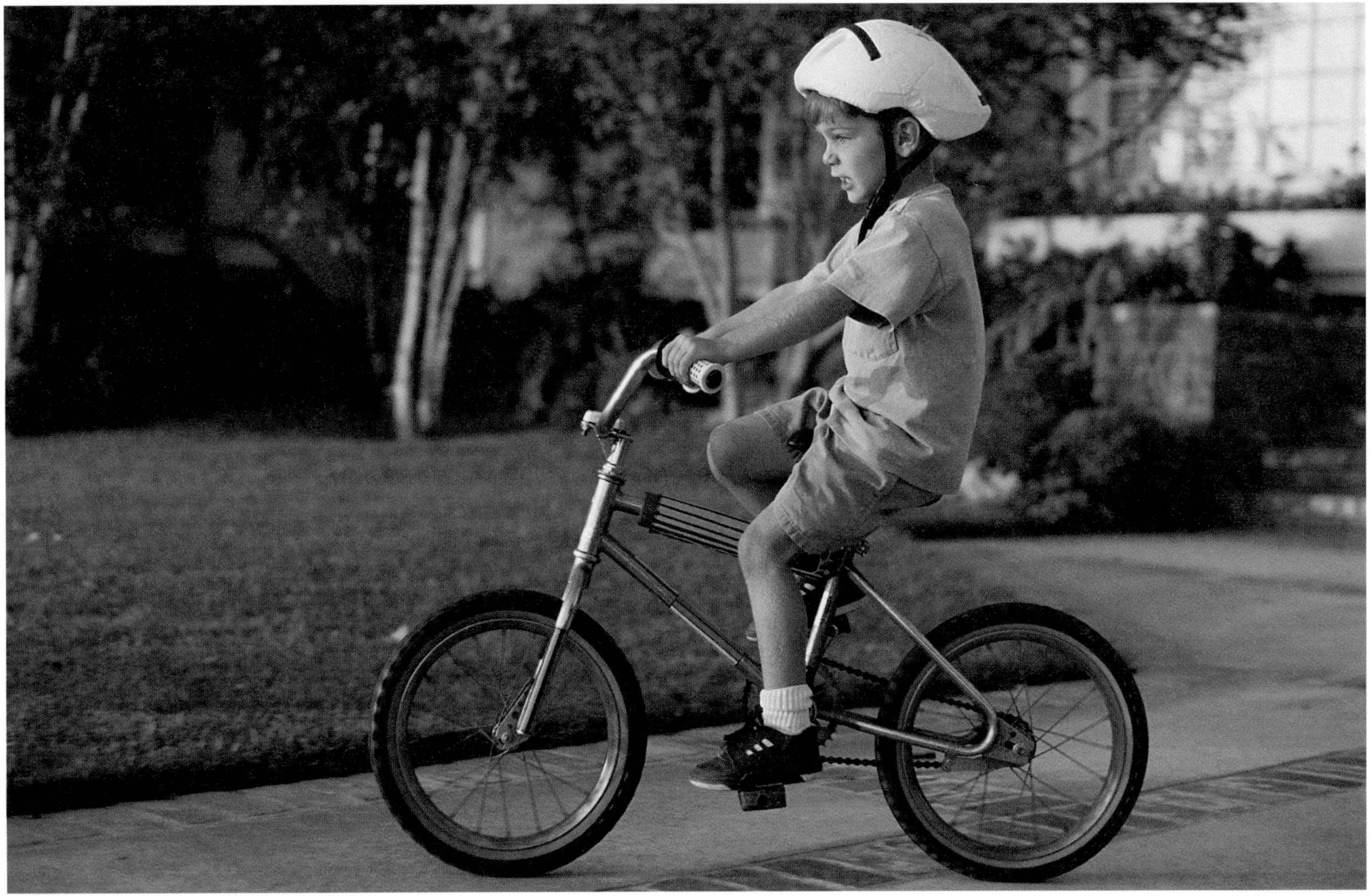

bike

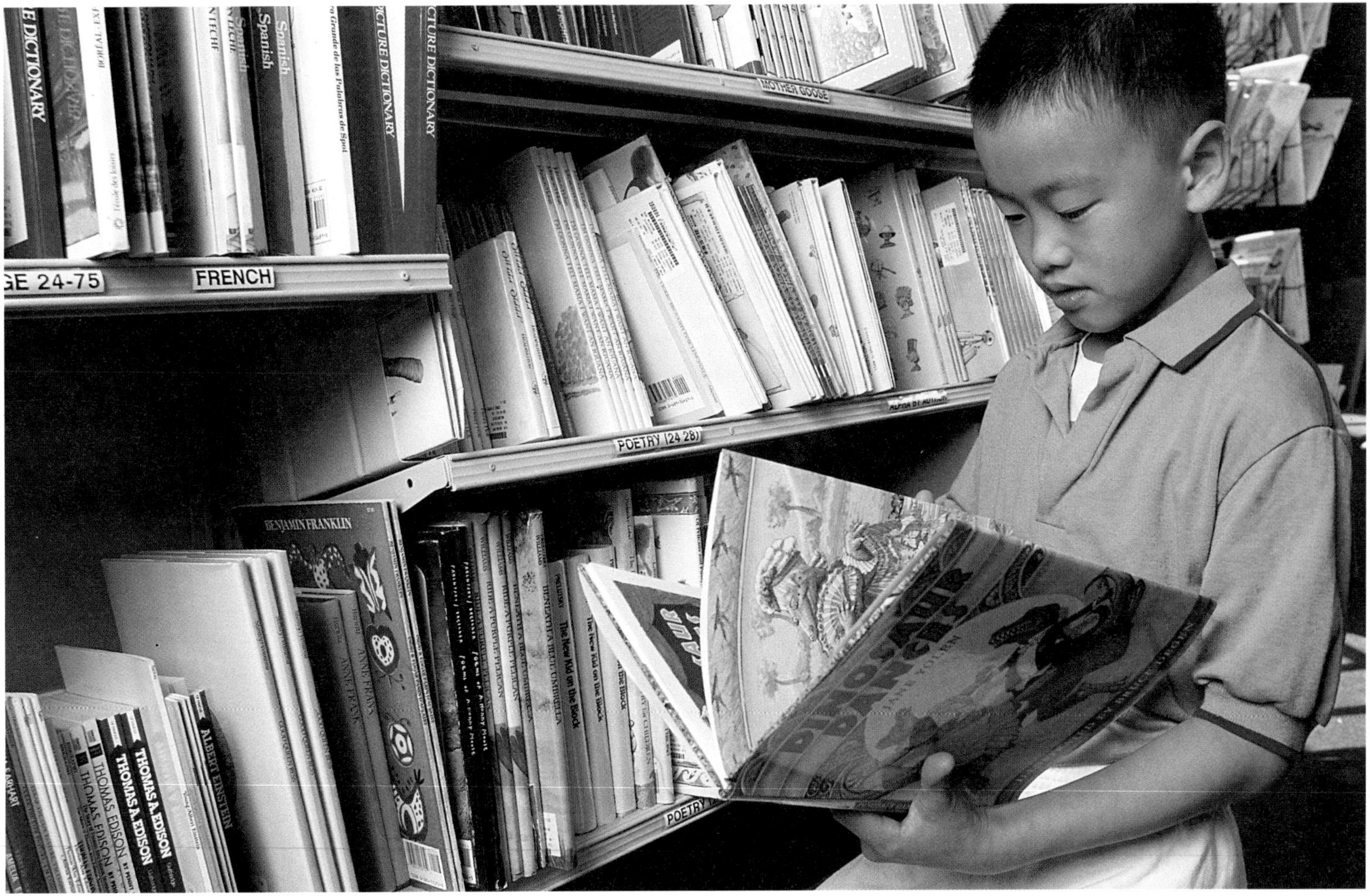
MOTHER GOOSE
PICTURE DICTIONARY
Spanish
GE 24-75
FRENCH
POETRY (24 28)
BENJAMIN FRANKLIN
THOMAS A. EDISON
THOMAS A. EDISON
ALBERT EINSTEIN
The New Kid on the Block
POETRY

books

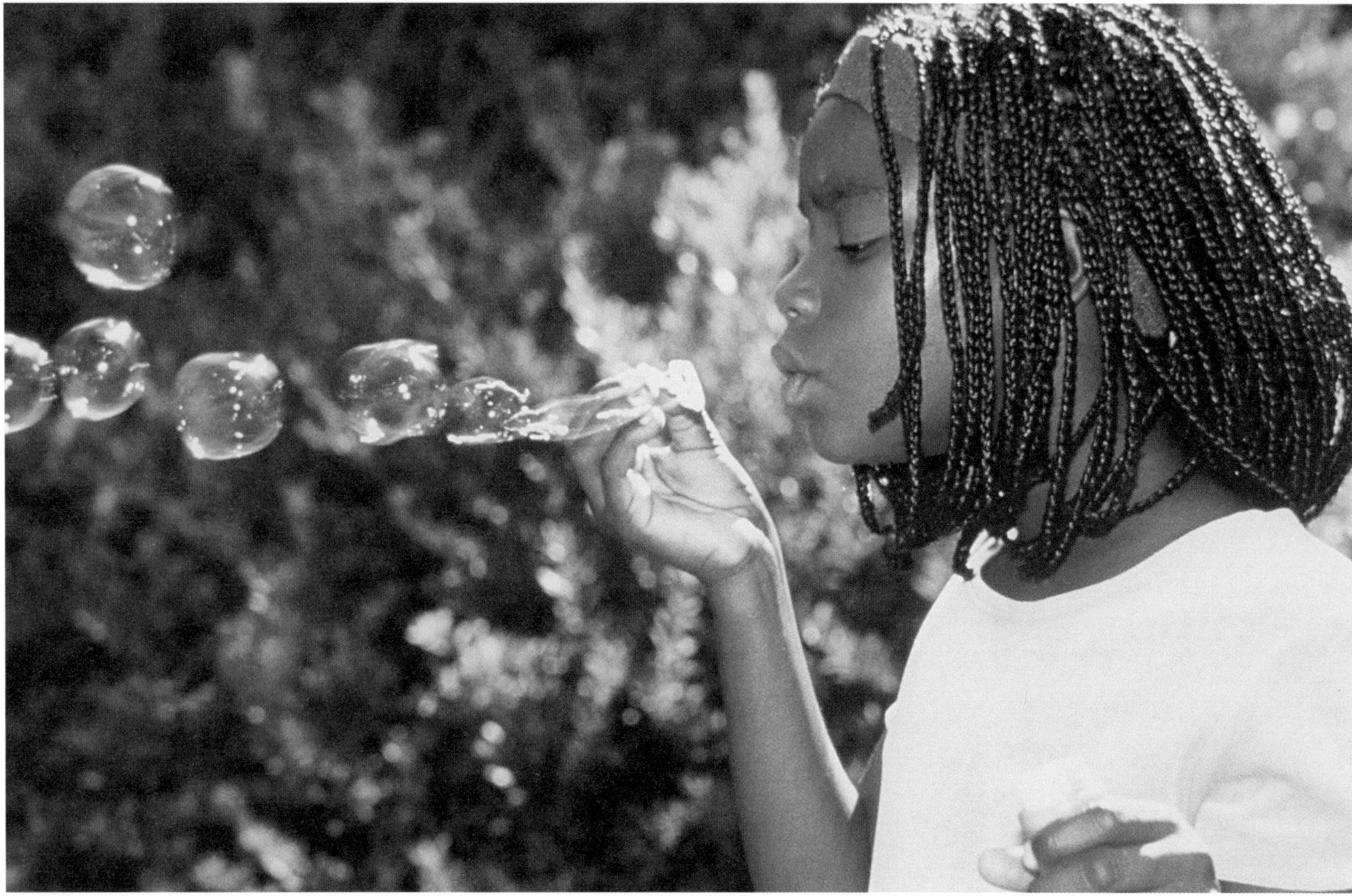

bubbles

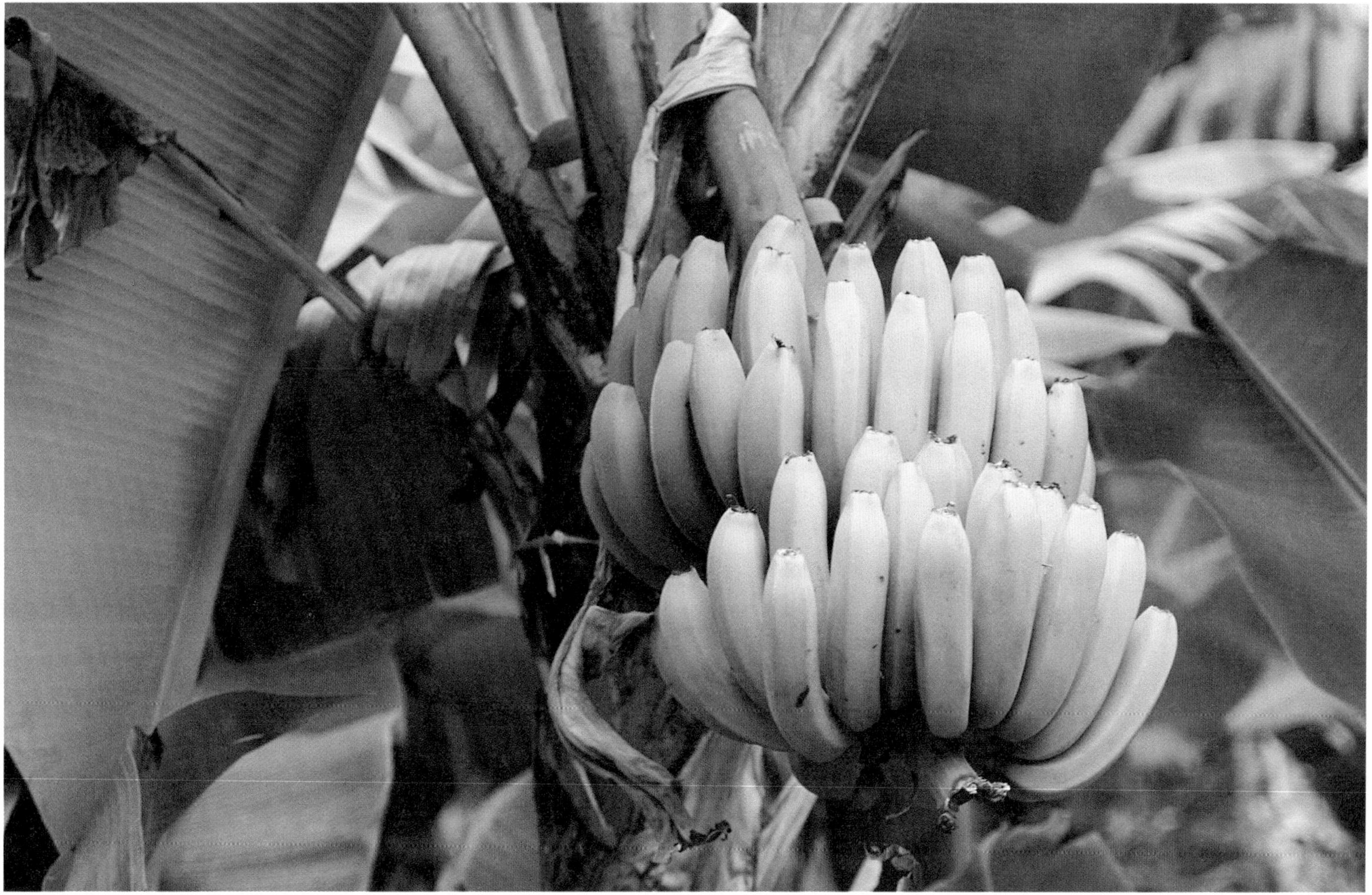

bananas

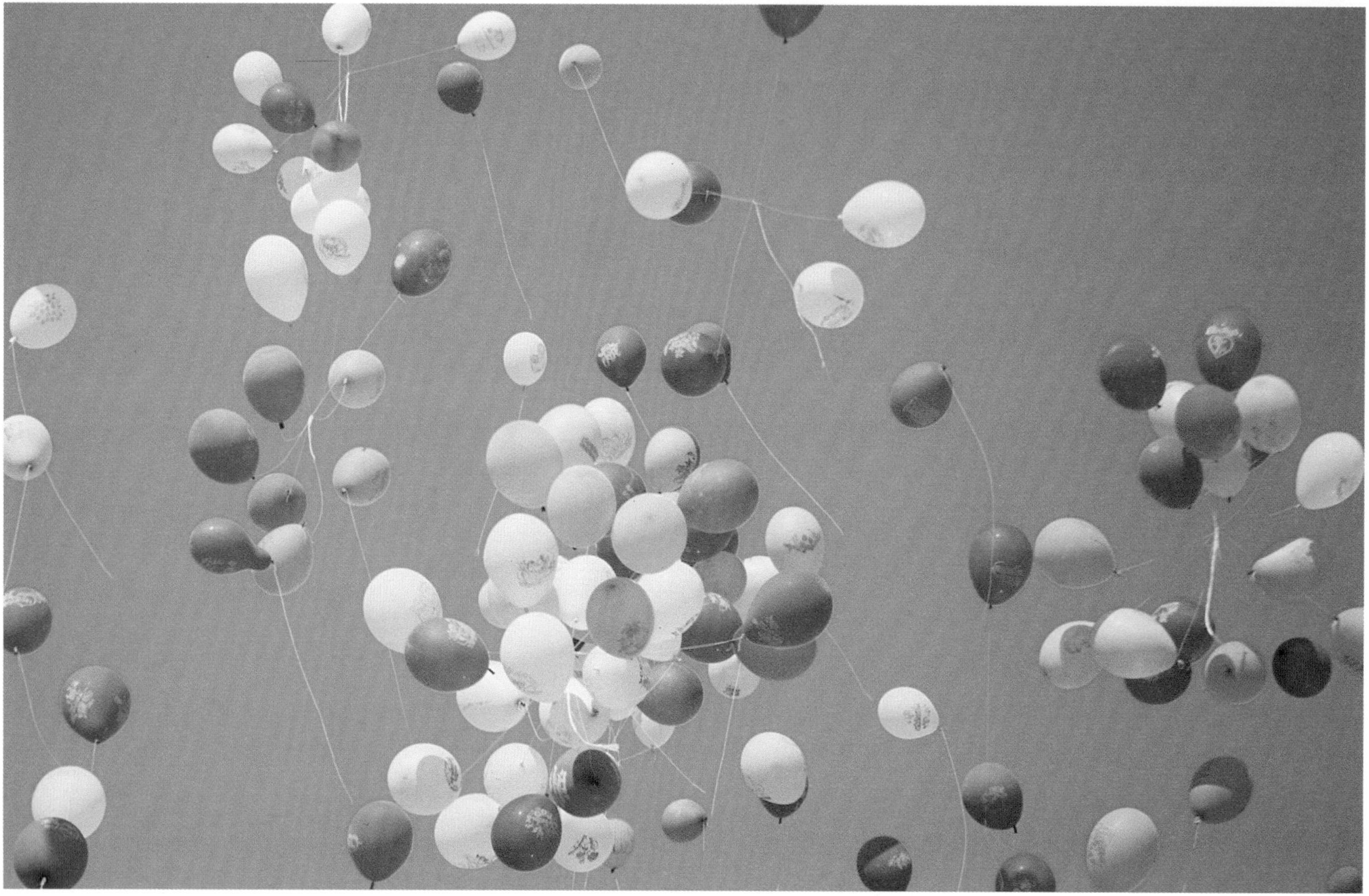

balloons